Know your Pet

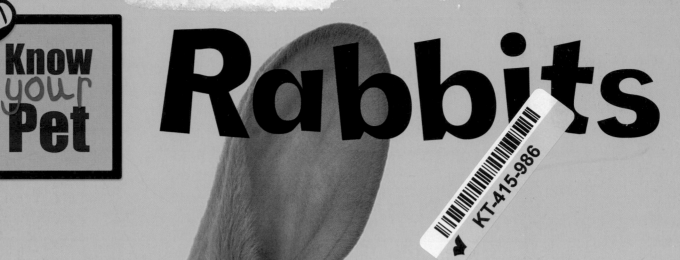

Rabbits

Michaela Miller

QED Publishing

First published in the UK in 2006 by
QED Publishing
A Quarto Group company
226 City Road
London EC1V 2TT
www.qed-publishing.co.uk

A Catalogue record for this book is available from the British Library.

ISBN 1 84538 500 4

Written by Michaela Miller
Consultant Chris Laurence, QVRM, TD, BCSc, MRCVS
Designed by Melissa Alaverdy
Editor Louisa Somerville
Pictures supplied by Warren Photographic

Publisher Steve Evans
Editorial Director Jean Coppendale
Art Director Zeta Davies

Printed and bound in China

Words in **bold** are explained in the glossary on page 30.

Contents

The right rabbit for you!

Rabbits may seem like easy pets to own because they're soft, cuddly and gentle but looking after them is a big responsibility. They need a rabbit friend to live with to be happy and lots of space to exercise as well.

Are rabbits for me?

To find out if rabbits are the right pets for you and your family, here are some questions to ask each other:

🐾 Are we prepared to give a home to more than one rabbit?

🐾 Can we afford to give our rabbits the biggest hutch and living space possible?

🐾 Can we give them a safe exercise area to play in?

🐾 Will we feed our rabbits twice a day, every day?

🐾 Are we prepared to clean out our rabbits' home regularly?

🐾 Can we afford to pay for the **vaccinations** and any other veterinary care our rabbits may need?

🐾 Will we make sure our rabbits are properly looked after when we go on holiday?

If you answered 'yes' to all the questions then rabbits could be just the pets for you!

Rabbits, rabbits, rabbits

Rabbits can be as small as Netherland Dwarfs, or as big as Flemish Giants, which can weigh up to 9.5kg. Rabbits have been bred over the years to have different characteristics. There are long-haired rabbits such as Angoras, which have woolly coats, and lop-eared rabbits, which have large, floppy ears.

A Flemish Giant rabbit shows off its magnificent ears.

Types of rabbit

There are three types of pure bred rabbits. Normal fur types have the same type of fur as wild rabbits. Rex and Satin rabbits have very short and dense fur. Fancy rabbits have all sorts of coats and features. Fancy rabbits are usually taken to rabbit shows by their owners and breeders, and are judged on their appearance.

A very fluffy Angora rabbit. Certain rabbits will not suit all owners. Long-haired rabbits need a lot of care – an Angora will need thorough grooming at least once a day. Very large rabbits, such as Flemish Giants, can be too heavy even for adults to lift.

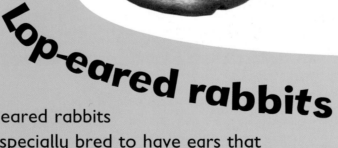

An English lop with enormous, floppy ears.

An adorable Dutch rabbit.

Lop-eared rabbits

Lop-eared rabbits are specially bred to have ears that hang down at the sides of their heads. Unlike most rabbits, lop-ears cannot prick up their ears to hear. Their ears are so long (about 17cm wide and up to 72cm long) they can't move around easily either. Their front claws must be trimmed to stop them scratching their ears as they move.

All pet rabbits are descended from wild European rabbits. They were probably bred for food as long ago as 600CE. Although pet rabbits come in many colours, all wild European rabbits look much the same. They have greyish brown coats on their upper bodies, white or light grey fur on their tummies and white tails.

Living together

Wild rabbits are social animals that live in groups. This is why pet rabbits are most happy living in pairs or groups. They can become lonely and depressed when kept on their own. Rabbit homes, called warrens, are made of underground burrows and tunnels. Rabbits sleep in the warren by day and come out to feed in the early morning and at dusk. Warrens are usually found on the edges of woodland around grassy areas and can contain as many as 30 rabbits. Each warren has a dominant male (**buck**) and also a dominant female (**doe**).

Rabbits use their tails to flash a warning signal to other rabbits when danger is about.

A doe can have three to seven litters of babies a year with up to eight **kittens** in each litter.

Rabbits prick up their ears to catch even the smallest sounds.

What do wild rabbits eat?

Rabbits' teeth are adapted to eat grasses, cereal crops and wild plants such as bramble, groundsel, chickweed and dandelion. They sometimes eat tree bark too. After a rabbit eats, the food comes out the other end only partly **digested**. The rabbit eats these droppings, which travel through its system again and come out as hard pellets – the rabbit's final droppings.

European wild rabbits were taken to Australia in the 1800s. Their population grew out of control because they had no natural predators.

Under attack

Wild rabbits depend on their coats to provide camouflage – if threatened they crouch low and keep still. When defending their territory, rabbits will often fight back. To make themselves look fierce, they flatten their ears and make their fur stand on end. They thump their back legs on the ground to warn other rabbits, and bite and kick whatever is threatening them. If pet rabbits are not happy being handled they will bite and kick, too.

Choosing your rabbits

If you decide to get rabbits, ask your vet to recommend good breeders or animal rescue centres in your area. Pet shops also sell rabbits, but it can be hard to find out about the rabbits' backgrounds. Pet shops sometimes put rabbits from different litters together, which can increase the risk of spreading disease.

Good homes

It is best to see the young rabbits you would like to buy with their mother. This way, you will be able to see if they come from a clean and disease-free environment, if they have been cared for properly and are used to being handled. The rabbits you choose should be around eight weeks old so that they will be easy to handle and to tame.

Rabbits need to live with other rabbits. It is unkind to keep one rabbit on its own, as it won't be happy.

A healthy pet

Healthy rabbits move with no signs of limping or soreness. When you hold the rabbit, run your hands over its body to check there are no wounds, lumps on its skin or bare patches. The rabbit's claws should be short and not torn at the ends. Its teeth should be clean and a normal length. Healthy rabbits will have no signs of diarrhoea – their droppings should be dry and round. A rabbit with a runny nose, sneezing or not breathing easily is probably ill.

A healthy rabbit has a clean coat, clear eyes and clean, pricked-up ears (unless it is a lop-ear).

Angoras

Angoras are one of the oldest rabbit breeds. They have wool rather than fur, which can grow up to 12cm long. Angoras need half an hour's brushing every day and regular clipping to keep their coats in good condition. In the summer, owners must take care that their angoras don't get heatstroke because of their thick coats. They can also suffer from hypothermia (getting too cold) if their fur gets wet and cold.

Rabbit and friend

It is unkind to keep one rabbit on its own. It is much better to give a home to a pair of rabbits, but make sure that you choose ones that can live together happily.

Who lives together?

Two or three female rabbits from the same litter will live together quite happily. Two male littermates can live together too, but they should be **neutered** to stop them fighting. Unneutered male and female rabbits should not be kept together. If you cannot give your rabbit a rabbit companion, then it can share a living area with poultry or tortoises.

A tortoise and a rabbit may get on surprisingly well together.

Rabbits and guinea pigs

Although you will sometimes see rabbits and guinea pigs living together, this is not a good idea. Unless the guinea pig and rabbit have been brought up together from a very young age, it is likely that the rabbit will bully and hurt the guinea pig. The best companion for a rabbit is another rabbit and the best companion for a guinea pig is another guinea pig.

New friends

If you have kept a pair of rabbits and one dies, the rabbit left behind will feel lonely. It's best to find it a new friend. Choose a young rabbit, but watch out in case it is bullied. Your new rabbit should be the same sex as the one that has died. Put the new rabbit in a cage next to the old one's. When they are used to each other, you can let them out together under supervision. Soon after this they can go in the same hutch, with part of it blocked off with a divider. Make a hole in the divider that only the young rabbit can fit through, so that it can go through to be on its own. After a while, if they have become good friends, they can live together without the divider.

Your rabbit is more likely to be friends with a young rabbit than an adult rabbit.

No babies, please!

It isn't a good idea to breed from your pet rabbits because there are already too many unwanted rabbits. The best way to stop rabbits breeding is not to keep male and female rabbits together. However, if you do keep male and female littermates together you should get them neutered or they will mate and have at least 24 babies a year. Many vets recommend that most female rabbits kept as pets should be neutered. Unneutered females are more at risk of getting infections and diseases.

Getting ready

Before you bring your rabbits home, you need somewhere for them to live. Your rabbits will need both a hutch and an exercise area where they can graze and play safely.

A ramp should lead from the hutch into an enclosed exercise area that is safe from predators and that the rabbits cannot burrow out of.

Home sweet home

Outdoor hutches should be weatherproof and raised off the ground to protect the rabbits from the damp and predators. The roof should be felted and slope backwards to let the rain run off. Your rabbits' home should be kept away from direct sunlight and wind. It needs two compartments – one for the daytime, with a mesh door that lets in light and one with a solid door where the rabbits can sleep at night and go when it is cold or wet. In very cold or hot weather, rabbits should be kept in indoor hutches and exercise areas, but not in a conservatory, greenhouse or garage.

A rabbit is usually frightened of anything that moves above its body because in the wild it may be attacked from above. When you play with your pet, approach it at its own level.

Right height?

Your rabbits' hutch should be high enough for each adult rabbit to stand up on its hind legs. It should also be long enough for all the rabbits to lie out at their full lengths at the same time, and to do two or three hops from one end to the other.

Sleep tight

Your rabbits' home will need proper bedding inside. Put a layer of newspaper on the floor of both compartments plus a layer of non-clumping cat litter and wood pulp about 5cm deep. The sleeping compartment will need a deep layer of straw or hay on top of the wood pulp. In colder weather, the rabbits will be happiest sleeping inside a whole bale of hay!

When the hutch is raised off the ground it makes it easier to clean.

No paint please

Paint can be poisonous to rabbits, so any painted bits of the hutch should not be near their living area. The outside of the hutch can be treated with a wood preservative to make it last longer, but the preservative used should be non-toxic and allowed to dry completely before the rabbits are put inside.

13

Eating and drinking

Pet rabbits cannot look for food on their own, as they would in the wild, if they live in a cage. So they depend on you to give them the right food and enough water to keep them healthy and happy.

Grass, hay, rabbit pellets and vegetables should all be part of your rabbits' diet.

The right diet

The best diet for rabbits is one that is similar to what they would eat in the wild — mostly grass (either fresh or freeze dried) and good-quality meadow hay. Keep hay for eating separate from hay used as bedding and put it in a hayrack in the hutch. Specially made **concentrated rabbit pellets** are available from pet shops. You can feed these to your rabbit in a heavy, earthenware pot that's easy to clean. Don't feed your rabbits more than the recommended amount, or you'll make them fat.

Green foods

Although rabbit pellets contain lots of vitamins and minerals, rabbits need other foods, too. In the wild they eat lots of greenery, so they'll like foods such as broccoli, cabbage, chicory, chard, parsley, watercress, celery leaves, dock, basil, kale, carrot and beetroot tops. If you can find wild plants, such as brambles, groundsel, chickweed and dandelions, these are good for rabbits, too. Not all wild plants are right for rabbits. Foxgloves, buttercups, celandines, toadflax, poppies, anemone, elder and bindweed are some of the plants that could poison your rabbits.

Dandelions are good for rabbits but not all wild plants are, so be careful what you give to your pet.

Rabbits need a mineral lick, which you can buy from a pet shop, attached to the hutch. This is a good way of ensuring that your pet gets the vitamins and minerals that it needs to stay healthy.

Killer weeds

Rabbits need to graze in an outdoor exercise area, but never let them graze anywhere that has been treated with weedkiller or **fertilizer**. These can be very poisonous to rabbits and could even kill them. You can collect wild plants for your rabbits, but make sure that you wash them thoroughly before you let your pets eat them.

Make sure that your rabbits always have lots of drinking water. A drip-feed water bottle with a metal spout, attached to the side of the hutch, is best as bowls of water can get quite dirty.

Grooming an handling

Handle young rabbits gently and frequently to get them used to being touched by people. A rabbit that's unused to human contact may bite, kick, scratch and try to escape when you hold it.

How to handle

The best way to pick up a rabbit is with both hands. Put one hand on the **scruff** of its neck and the other under its bottom, supporting its back legs. Cradle the rabbit securely against your body. Its head can rest on your shoulder. Never pick a rabbit up by its ears or just by the scruff of the neck. To return your rabbit to its hutch, hold it in both hands against your body, support its feet and gently place it inside. Always put your rabbit inside from the front of the hutch, never lower it in from above.

Support your rabbit's feet and legs when you're holding it, so it won't kick.

Regular grooming

Short-haired rabbits are good at keeping themselves clean and looking after their own fur, so they don't need daily grooming. However, it's a good idea to groom them regularly because it means you get to know your rabbits well and they get used to being handled. Use a medium-stiff brush to remove loose hairs and dead skin.

Brush from the rabbit's head towards its bottom, never the other way round.

Health check

Grooming gives you the chance to check your rabbit for lumps, bumps and bare patches on its skin. You can also check for fleas and mites, which live in its ears. Look out for **fly strike**, which is when a fly lays its eggs in dirty areas around a rabbit's bottom. This is most likely to happen during warm weather, when rabbits are kept in dirty conditions or if they are too fat to groom themselves properly.

Long claws

If your rabbit's claws grow too long and split, they should be clipped to stop it getting sore paws. Ask your vet to clip the claws the first time and show you and the adult in charge of your pet what to do. The vet will clip the claws straight across using special animal nail clippers.

To take your rabbits to the vet, you will need a secure, well-ventilated carrier that they cannot chew their way out of.

Looking after the hutch

To keep your rabbits happy and healthy, their home must be clean and well looked after. By nature, rabbits are clean animals. If they live in dirty surroundings they can become distressed and get ill.

Keeping it clean

Rabbits tend to use one spot in their hutch as a toilet. This place should be cleaned every day and the floor litter replaced. You may find that if you put a litter tray here the rabbits will use it as their toilet. This means you only have to clean out the tray to keep the toilet area clean.

🐾 Once or twice a week, sweep all the floor litter into a bucket and take out the newspaper lining the floor. Replace with fresh litter and newspaper.

🐾 Replace the bedding every 10–14 days.

🐾 Wash out the rabbits' water bottle daily and their food bowl every few days.

🐾 Keep your rabbits' exercise area clean, too.

🐾 Three or four times a year, scrape out, wash and disinfect the hutch with suitable products. Check with your vet or pet shop for rabbit-safe brands. Rinse everything thoroughly and allow to dry before the rabbits are put back inside.

A litter tray placed inside the hutch can make cleaning out the hutch a much easier task.

Fresh grazing

Portable runs should be moved around the garden to make sure the rabbits always have fresh grazing. Once the grass has been nibbled away, sprinkle the area lightly with lawn lime. Don't move the rabbits back until the grass has completely grown up again. Only let your rabbits graze in the same spot two or three times a year, otherwise they could become ill.

Rabbits need a safe exercise area and somewhere to graze. They also need somewhere to hide if they get frightened, such as an upturned cardboard box.

Too hot

Rabbits can easily suffer heatstroke, so outdoor rabbit hutches and exercise areas should never be in direct sunlight. Don't shut your rabbits in their hutch on warm days. They need a safe, shady exercise area in which to graze and play, and access to the hutch if they want it. In very warm climates, they should be housed inside in the cool.

Introduce pet cats and dogs to your rabbits slowly and carefully, so they don't frighten your rabbit. If your rabbit starts to behave as if it is frightened, stop the training and try again later with the dog or cat further away.

Dogs and rabbits

To introduce your new rabbit to your dog, you need a quiet room and the help of the adult who is responsible for the dog's training. Each introductory session should last about five to ten minutes.

If your dog is the sort that tries to chase small animals such as rabbits, squirrels, birds and cats, it may treat your pets in the same way. The dog must be kept away from them if the training doesn't work.

Cats and rabbits

Cats and rabbits often become good friends. But never forget that your cat is a hunter, and it may attack a small rabbit.

Cats and rabbits often get along together if they are introduced properly in a quiet room. Keep the rabbit in its cage with the door shut and let the cat sniff around it. Stay in the room with them. Then take the cat out of the room and let the rabbit out of its cage. Let it sniff around to get used to the room. After a couple of weeks' training, you'll be able to open the door of the rabbit's cage and see how the cat and rabbit behave together. Be ready to separate them if either looks unhappy or aggressive. Never leave them alone together.

Training sessions

🐾 Put the rabbit in a carrying cage with the door shut, staying close by. The adult keeps the dog on its lead and gives the usual commands "sit" and "stay". When the dog obeys, give it a treat. If the dog looks at the rabbit rather than the adult, give it a treat to get its attention. If this fails, take it out of the room and try again later.

🐾 When the dog is settled, bring it on its lead towards the rabbit's carrying cage so the dog can sniff around it. Reward it for good behaviour and obeying the commands "sit" and "stay".

🐾 Next, the adult takes the dog to the other side of the room on its lead and makes sure it obeys commands. Take the rabbit out of its cage and sit on the floor and let it move about. The adult rewards the dog if it stays still. The dog and rabbit should not be allowed to sniff each other yet.

🐾 Over several days you should be able to let the dog and rabbit move closer together, but don't let the dog off its lead in case it lunges at the rabbit. You could put a muzzle on the dog for this stage. Make sure the room has hiding places out of the dog's reach, where the rabbit can go if it feels threatened.

🐾 The final stage is when the dog and rabbit can be together safely in a room, but always supervised. Never leave them alone together.

Even if your dog and rabbit look like the best of friends, they should never be left alone together.

The house rabbit

Rabbits are so sociable that if they are looked after properly and given the right place to live they can make very good and happy house pets.

Indoor homes

You could have a special room for your rabbits with a hutch and exercise area, or use a large wire crate and put a litter tray inside. Cover the floor of the cage with synthetic sheepskin, carpet, lino, towels or newspaper. You can train your rabbits to use a litter tray by putting it in their home with some of their droppings in it. The hutch will also need a hayrack, a water bottle and a feeding bowl. Keep the hutch out of draughts, and away from direct sunlight and radiators, to stop your pets getting too hot. Rabbits can get stressed by loud noises, so keep the hutch away from televisions and music systems.

Rabbits can live very happily indoors. Make sure they have a safe area in which to live, play and exercise.

Keeping safe

Whether you keep your rabbits in one room or let them hop about more freely, be aware of their safety. If your rabbits are in a room with an open fireplace, use a fireguard. Don't leave them on their own where there is wooden furniture or carpets that they might chew. Rabbits can easily fall down stairs, so use a stair guard to stop your rabbits climbing up the stairs. Don't let rabbits into the kitchen or leave them unsupervised with other pets, such as cats and dogs.

Keep rabbit rooms free of houseplants, as many plants are dangerous to rabbits.

Rabbits and utility rooms

Don't keep your rabbits in a utility room because the room can get overheated and noisy. There may be cables about that your rabbits could chew and they could try to get into the empty washing machine, too.

Chewing a cable could kill your rabbit.

Make sure electrical cables are out of your rabbits' reach so that they cannot chew them.

Playing with your rabbits

Rabbits are naturally active – they need exercise and things to do. It's unfair to keep them in their hutches for long periods during the day. You don't have to spend much on equipment – there are simple ways to help your rabbits have fun.

Fun toys

Playing with a rabbit when it's very young helps you become friends. Put some cardboard boxes filled with hay in the exercise area for the rabbits to burrow and hide in. You could join several boxes together and cut holes in the sides big enough for your rabbits to go through. Rabbits like old towels to hide under as well. Kitchen and toilet roll tubes are simple toys that they can roll about.

Rabbits will love climbing in and out of different holes in your cardboard warren.

Rabbit games

Some rabbits will happily roll jingly play balls and even footballs about! You can buy special rabbit play balls from pet shops, which you can fill with alfalfa pellets or other treats. As the rabbit rolls it about the treats start to fall out. You can teach a rabbit to play hide-and-seek. Let your rabbit see you hide a treat in your hand. Go and hide behind something. When the rabbit finds you, give it the treat.

Flowerpots lying on their sides make good bolt holes. To stop the pots rolling about, stabilize each side with a stone or brick.

Playing safely

The best way to play with rabbits is on the floor, on their level. Sit on the floor and roll a ball or a tube towards your pet. Eventually it may roll or toss it back to you. Rabbits have fragile spines and can be badly injured or die if they fall. Never play with them on sofas, tables, chairs or on any other surface from which they could fall.

Get your rabbits used to playing by getting down on the floor with them.

Health check

The vet is an important source of care advice for your rabbits. Find a local vet by looking in the phone book or by asking friends and neighbours who have pets to recommend vets in the area.

Check-ups

Most vets will recommend that you bring your rabbits for check-ups once a year. They will be checked for overgrown teeth and claws and for parasites such as fleas, lice and mites. You should always take a rabbit to the vet if you think it is unwell. Signs of ill health to look out for include:

- Runny eyes, noses and ears
- Breathing difficulties
- Diarrhoea
- Skin problems
- Limping
- Not wanting to eat
- Lack of energy

Disease free

When you first get your rabbits take them to the vet for a health check. Your rabbits should be vaccinated against Viral Haemorrhagic Disease, a deadly infection that can spread quickly from rabbit to rabbit. Owners who have handled an infected rabbit can pass this disease to other rabbits, too. If your rabbits will live outdoors or near wild rabbits, your vet may recommend vaccination against Myxomatosis — another deadly disease carried by fleas and other insects.

Long in the tooth

If a rabbit is not given things to gnaw on, its teeth will get too long and it will be in pain and unable to open and shut its mouth properly. Your vet will need to trim its teeth to make your pet more comfortable. Apart from hard food to eat, rabbits need a gnawing block in their hutch and exercise area. Branches from apple trees (if they haven't been treated with pesticides) are good for rabbits to chew.

Root vegetables, such as carrots, parsnips and turnips are good for your rabbits' teeth, as are stems of kale and Brussels sprouts.

Caring for elderly rabbits

Elderly rabbits usually need special care to make sure they stay fit and healthy for as long as possible. Rabbits that are properly cared for usually live for eight to 12 years (although they may live to 16 years). Rabbits that don't get enough exercise tend to have shorter lives.

Extra care

Older rabbits can easily get ill, so take extra care that their home, exercise and toilet areas are clean and dry and that there is hay and bedding for them to burrow into. Older rabbits tend to gain weight, which can make them unhealthy. Make sure their diet includes lots of hay and grass.

An elderly rabbit will need to have its teeth checked regularly by a vet to make sure that they are in good condition and are not overgrown.

Vet checks

Older rabbits can develop problems with teeth, hearing, sight and lumps on their skin. Take your rabbit to the vet for a check-up at least once a year and make sure its vaccinations are up to date. The vet will check your pet's teeth and claws to make sure they aren't overgrown and painful. Your vet may also prescribe medicine for arthritis – a disease that can make your rabbit's leg joints ache.

Saying goodbye

If your pet is very ill or in pain you may have to have it put down. The vet can give it an injection so that it dies painlessly. Afterwards you can leave its body at the vet's or bring it home to bury. Your vet may cremate your pet so that you can scatter the ashes. It is very sad when a pet dies. You may find it helpful to write a story, look at photos or make a scrapbook about your pet's life.

When a rabbit is about five or six years old it may move about more slowly and spend longer times just sitting or lying in its favourite place.

Pet cemeteries

Some people like to bury their pet in a proper pet cemetery – your vet may be able to give you details or you could look on the internet to find your nearest one. There are also virtual cemeteries online where you can buy an online grave in your rabbit's name with a donation going to an animal welfare charity. Many people find a special place in their own garden to bury their pet. You could have a small ceremony to say goodbye.

Glossary

Buck A male rabbit

Concentrated rabbit pellets Food available from pet shops containing the correct balance of vitamins, minerals, fibre and other ingredients rabbits need to be healthy, as well as grass or hay

Digestion The process by which food is broken down inside the body

Doe A female rabbit

Domestic animal An animal tamed and kept by humans

Fertilizer A chemical that is put in the soil or directly on plants to make them grow more quickly. Fertilizers are poisonous to rabbits

Fly strike When flies lay eggs on a dirty rabbit. As the eggs hatch, the grubs burrow into the rabbit's skin to feed

Lop-eared rabbits Rabbits that have been bred so that their ears droop and drag on the ground and cannot be pricked up

Kitten A baby rabbit

Neuter An operation to stop rabbits breeding

Scruff The loose skin around a rabbit's neck

Vaccination An injection that can prevent an animal catching a disease

Index

Notes for parents

General notes

The adults in the family are responsible for the welfare of the rabbits in their care and the safety of children around them.

Be certain that you can afford all the necessary veterinary and housing costs before you buy rabbits as pets.

Rabbit hutches should be as large as possible – many hutches sold in pet shops are far too small. Rabbits are also highly social animals and it is unfair to keep one by itself or to confine your rabbits to a hutch for most of the day.

It is best not to breed the rabbits you keep as pets. A pair of breeding rabbits can have as many as 24 kittens a year.

When you go away on holiday you will need to make plans for your rabbits. There are boarding establishments which look after rabbits, or you may have a reliable friend or neighbour who will check on your rabbits twice a day, feed them, let them out for exercise and shut them up safely at night.

If you choose to add you pet to an online virtual cemetery after its death, check that the website is legitimate and that all financial transactions are secure.

Safety checklist

- Although domesticated rabbits look cute and cuddly they instinctively behave very much like their wild relatives. This means they can be aggressive and will bite, scratch and kick if not trained to be handled when they are young. Children should wear long-sleeved shirts when handling them and be well supervised.

- Rabbits that do not want to be handled will start to struggle and should be put down gently.

- All children and adults in the family should be taught to handle rabbits properly.

- Rabbits should never be picked up by the ears or by the scruff of the neck as this can cause them pain and distress and they may dislocate their spines if they kick hard.

- Larger rabbits, such as Flemish Giants, are very heavy and are not suitable for children to lift and carry about.

- Rabbits can be badly hurt and may die if they are dropped or fall off furniture or down stairs. The best way to play with them is on the ground, on their level.